W

Time to Leave

When it's Time to Leave, is a guide to help you accept death and see it as a natural step on the eternal journey of life. It is written to comfort those who are there to support, love and render care.

Dr. Jim Turrell

When it's Time to Leave
By Dr. Jim Turrell
Copyright 2014 by Dr. Jim Turrell
All rights reserved

Published by HeartTalk
Costa Mesa, CA

ISBN: 978-0-9667986-2-3

Printed in the United States of America
Second Edition, July 2015

All rights reserved. Except as permitted by applicable copyright laws, no part of this book may be reproduced, duplicated, sold or distributed in any form or by any means, either mechanical, by photocopy, electronic, or by computer, or stored in a database or retrieval system, without the express written permission of the publisher/authors, except for brief quotations by reviewers.

This is a work of non-fiction. The ideas presented are those of the author alone. All references to possible results to be gained from the techniques discussed in this book relate to specific past examples and are not necessarily representative of any future results specific individuals may achieve.

Foreword

Death is a point of departure. It is the place where we wait for that moment when called out of the *human condition* we transcend and re-form ourselves into the *spiritual experience*. Whatever you had on the schedule is no longer relevant. Whatever you needed to do…it's unimportant.

Very few people think about death and how to process the experience of dying. When death happens, they get hammered by feelings of helplessness, lost in what feels like a forest of meaningless emotions. Meaningless does not mean unimportant. It means you are being forced to process feelings you've never had to think about—unfamiliar feelings of which you have no information. This book gives you the information to process the experience and clarify the confusion. It shows you by example and lesson ways to think and reason.

This book is intentionally brief. It is written to maximize what the author believes to be essential information necessary to stabilize the uncertainty and create the confidence that enables one to move through this experience.

You will learn:

- The mechanics of grief
- How to understand death
- How to break the news to others
- Tools to mitigate uncertainty and fear
- Who is in charge? What kind of decisions must they make?
- What to talk about. How to listen. What is important?
- What creates clarity and what creates confusion
- Why the fear of life is more difficult than the fear of death
- The one thing guaranteed to remove fear
- How to honor other belief systems
- A way to pray that will bring you peace and give you confidence
- What needs to be healed and how to heal
- The five keys to being prepared for a death in the family

- Patience, Compassion and Love
- What is Hospice? What is Palliative Care?
- What to say. How to share. How to listen.
- How you handle hospital visits and being in the room when someone dies
- How to react when the patient starts seeing dead relatives
- How to say goodbye and the final curtain
- Why memorials are important and an example of how to organize one

Introduction

There is a story that John Matteson writes in his Pulitzer Prize winning book about Louisa May Alcott and her father Bronson. Louisa May was famous for her mid-19th-century book, *Little Women*. Bronson Alcott was known as one of the early Transcendentalists and friends with Ralph Waldo Emerson and Henry David Thoreau. The book examines their relationship and tells the story of their deaths.

Bronson was failing in health and had called Louisa May to his beside. In their conversation he invited Louisa May to come with him when he died. Louisa, who had never married and was by all accounts healthy, declined his offer and returned to Boston. In less than 48 hours Louisa May came down with a fever and died.

Few are prepared for death and most keep it at bay by ignoring its inevitable possibility. Could Louisa May Alcott have predicted her own demise? Probably not. When we hear the news about a friend, or a loved one dying or we ourselves get the news of our impending expiration, we are generally not prepared. Death is the ultimate change agent. Death has a domino effect that sets off many chain reactions, most of which are an emotional reflex based on fear and lack of knowledge.

I have been a minister for 30 years. I have witnessed death and helped many walk out of the shadow cast by our fears and uncertainty about death.

My book is an examination of how the process works and how you can prepare yourself for this experience. I wrote this book for those who have received their expiration notice and the friends and family who will ultimately support them. It is a brief book that can give you a different way to think about death and help you understand grief, loss, healing, and the reason for memorials. I have put a copy of the memorial service I use at the end of this book. There are many variations.

I suggest you look over the table of contents and start with any chapter heading that you think would be helpful.

Contents

Foreword iii
You will learn: v
Introduction vii
Chapter 1 The Truth About Death 1
  How did you get the news? 2
  Who is in charge? 3
  Where do you want this to happen? 8
Chapter 2 The Fear of Death or The Fear of Life 13
  The context of your belief is the key 13
  You do not have to compromise 17
  Honoring the process of what you believe 20
Chapter 3 Prayers 23
  Peace of Mind 23
  What needs to be healed? 25
  Prayers that light the way, deepen your faith, take away the fear, and focus you on peace 26
Chapter 4 Family and Friends 33
  Have no expectation 33
  Patience, Compassion, and Love 36
  Hospice 41
  Palliative Care 42
  The Quality of Life 43
Chapter 5 What to Say and How to Listen 45
  Listen first then what to share 45

 What to ask when you don't know the person or much about their history or condition................ 46
 Conversations with older folks 49
 Family Dynamics 52
 Finding balance and peace of mind in the process of grief.. 53
 On seeing dead people 56
 Saying goodbye and the final curtain 58

Chapter 6 Passing Through: Stories of Transformation 63
 Louis O. 63
 Dimensional prayer 66
 Learn to pray 68
 Suzie V. 69
 Learn the Law of Cause and Effect............ 72
 Patty P. 74
 Learn to love and trust the life you've been given to live.. 76

Chapter 7 Suicide 79
 The Truth about Suicide............................. 79
 Do Not Resuscitate ~ Jan's Story............... 80
 The Self-Inflicted Suicide ~ Three Case Studies....... 82
 Does suicide make death a different experience?..... 87
 For those who have suffered the loss a loved one and are still trying to figure out why 88
 A Philosophy of Healing 90
 If you've lost a loved one to suicide........... 91

Chapter 8 The Memorial, The Memory, The Miracle.. 95
  Who is the memorial for? 95
  What needs to happen at the memorial? 97
  The Miracle ~ 30, 60, 90, 120 Days Out 100
Chapter 9 The Memorial Service 105
  Music and introduction of immediate family 105
  Statement of Truth 106
  Gibran on Death 106
  The 23rd Psalm 106
  Eulogies, sharing and music 107
  Minister's healing message 108
  Release 108
   Closing song, prayer or ask the attendees to say the Lord's Prayer aloud. 109
  More programs by Dr. Jim Turrell 110

"I'm not afraid of death;
I just don't want to be there when it happens."
—**Woody Allen**

Chapter 1
The Truth About Death

Death is not a sentence. It is the knowledge of transformation guiding us to the next experience. Humanity struggles with eternality because it cloaks the infinite in space and time…then stamps it with an expiration date. Knowledge about Transformation provides spiritual scope and range that redefine the experience of death as we move out of the human condition into a spiritual condition. There is no end to what we are becoming and there is no death.

Time to Leave

How did you get the news?

Eventually everyone has to get the news about death. When I changed careers in 1984 and moved to Florida, my mom and dad came from California to visit. Mom was complaining about stomach pains. She thought it was diverticulitis. However, when she got back home, my sister called and said that mom had a biopsy on her stomach and the doctor walked into her hospital room and said, "You have cancer and it has spread throughout your body. You have a few months, I suggest you put your affairs in order." Then he walked out of the room. The death of a parent is not easy, even though millions of parents die every year around the world in every country, city, village, and town.

My family was in shock. My mom went through a heavy chemo treatment and I flew back to see her and was trying hard to figure out how to look at her 80-pound body, drawn face, and strange wig. I decided to look at her eyes. It was the only part of her body that was still the same. She was tired and putting on her best game face. I wondered, "Would this be our final conversation."

She smiled when she was through talking, got up and was humming a tune and sort of shuffled her feet as she went back to bed. I got in my car and drove to my hotel and stopped the car about halfway there and cried for a good 20 to 30 minutes.

Grief is an odd combination of news and waiting to see how things play out. Hardly any of us are prepared for the feelings of helplessness, the conversations about memorials, and the opinions, good-will and sadness everyone is trying to process. But you process it. Things get organized. And it all revolves around one question: Who is in charge?

Who is in charge?
For the Patient

Expiration dates are not easy to hear. Delivering bad news is equally difficult. So let's look at a way to absorb and process the news.

People react first from their emotions. The usual reaction is fear and uncertainty. It ranges from feeling like a helpless child to raging like an angry bull. If you are unprepared you can be overwhelmed for a time and have no idea how to think or respond. You feel lost, displaced, evicted, thrown out of your routine, and abandoned by any sense of being normal. So how do you prepare to hear this kind of news?

It takes focus and practice to prepare your mind to handle it. You need a logical way to look at how you function in relation to your *higher power*. Most people call their higher power God. Many people see God as an outside power and death a very conditional experience.

God is the power within and encompasses all. God is in us and we are in God. There is *no separation* between God and us. When you see Life and God as One, you will see death as a transition from one form of life to another. But there is a difference between having the faith *of* God versus having faith *in* God. Faith is a mental faculty that once convinced of its oneness with God, helps you see Life as a *unified, eternal, and constantly changing experience that unfolds and emerges as we grow.*

To understand death as a normal transition helps to dismantle doubt. It opens you up to learn about love's ability to cast out fear and your capacity to love yourself and others. A lot of people talk about love. Many acknowledge its power to change lives. Few, however, use love to focus their intentions and discipline their behavior. Love is a truth that influences how you think and react. When you come from love, you seek to understand and to be understood. When you come from fear, you seek to dominate and resist change.

So how do you learn to understand love as a way to cast out fear? One way is to work with affirmations.

The Truth About Death

An affirmation is a brief statement of truth that you write down and frequently read aloud. The reason you repeat affirmations about the *eternality of life* is to train your mind to think different about death, to be prepared to tell yourself the truth, especially while you're listening to a doctor tell you the facts about your expiration date.

You repeat an affirmation, not because you're trying to make it true; you repeat it because it is true.

One of my favorite affirmations is, *One in conscious unity with God constitutes a majority.* Here are several more affirmations that you can start training with: (Instructions: pick one affirmation and copy it to a 3 x 5 card. Keep it with you and say it aloud every hour, making a mark on your card every time you say it. If you do this every hour, you will begin to feel a powerful sense of renewal and faith. This is the work that creates miracles.)

1. I am part of the unified whole. My life is eternal and part of a vast sacred substance which is constantly changing form. Death is not the end; it is my transformation into a greater experience of love.

2. As I see God as the whole, perfect and complete idea of life, I see myself as the avenue through which a great good is moving. My transformation confirms my oneness with God.

3. Today I am focused on God's Love. I see God's Love as the experience of compassion, trust and faith guiding me to a greater understanding of the eternal.

For Family and Friends

Very few people think about death and how to process the experience of a loved one dying. As a result, many family and friends get hammered by feelings of helplessness, lost in what feels like a forest of meaningless emotions. Meaningless does not mean unimportant. It means you are being forced to process feelings you've never had to think about—unfamiliar feelings of which you have no information, information that could help you assign meaning to the circumstance. Instead, the information is noise. It feels illogical. It threatens your routine. Whatever you had on the schedule is no longer relevant. Whatever you needed to do…it's unimportant.

I've counseled hundreds of folks in the process of losing a loved one. Slowly they work their way through the feelings of helplessness. Gradually, they begin to attach meaning to death, and inevitably three realizations emerge:

1. This is not their death.
2. They are not in charge.
3. No matter how unfair and unimaginable it feels this circumstance is out of their control.

The Truth About Death

You are *not* in charge of the patient's feelings, fears, or treatment or how they choose to process this experience and the decisions they make. You are in charge of listening, helping, serving, and praying.

When it is time for you to leave, you will be in charge. Until that time, the transformation set into motion is an inevitable consequence of decisions that have already been made.

Will you be prepared to accept this?

Some prepare themselves, most don't. For those who are prepared, the process is a gradual acceptance. The prepared person slowly abandons the human condition and shifts their focus to the eternal journey. The best way to be prepared is to load up your subconscious with statements of truth that automatically respond and keep you calm and focused on living. For many, this makes the last weeks, months or years of life a rich experience of gratitude and joy. Family members and friends can also practice writing and saying life affirming affirmations. Then, as their roles unfold and transformation happens, death becomes a lesson in compassion.

Remember, you're not trying to make the affirmation true; you repeat it because it is true.

Here are several affirmations written specifically for care givers: (Instructions: pick one affirmation and

Time to Leave

copy it to a 3 x 5 card. Keep it with you and say it aloud every hour, making a mark on your card every time you say it. If you do this every hour, you will begin to feel a powerful sense of renewal and faith. This is the work that creates miracles.)

1. The nature of life is on-going, eternal, and constantly changing. Death is not the end. It is the transformation of the Spirit into a new and vital form.

2. My life is filled with opportunities to practice being the agent of love. Today, I am that agent of love and acceptance. All is well and unfolding as it should.

3. My part in _____ (write in the name of the patient) transformation is to listen, pray and accept God's guidance and love.

Where do you want this to happen?

Think about this and decide.

I was working with a long-time congregant. She had just been diagnosed with a return of cancer to her lungs and it had spread to her brain. She was hoping to get four more months to enjoy her grandkids. The next week, however, she suffered some serious seizures and went into the hospital and was given some powerful drugs that would put her into a coma-like state.

She accepted the drugs but refused to stay in the hospital. She decided to go home. She knew if she stayed in the hospital, they would have hydrated her with an I.V., put a tube in her lungs to drain away any fluids and probably given her medication to keep her blood pressure up. She made peace with her experience, went home and passed with the help of a hospice nurse, family and friends.

The experience is different for each, and I would not want anyone to leave a hospital if that is what they truly wanted. I have seen many go to a hospital and pass peacefully and many go home and pass peacefully. What is important is that you, the patient, make the choice.

Once I was asked to visit a patient who was dying at home. I walked into a family room and he was in a bed facing a wall. Behind him was a window overlooking a beautiful garden, attended by humming birds and big yellow bees.

I didn't know why he was facing the wall. There was a lot of confusion in the room. Some were trying to encourage him to live and some saw him as in the process of making his transition. I asked him what he wanted. He wasn't sure, in part because of the confusion around him and, in part, because he had not made a decision. He wasn't prepared.

I encouraged him to be alive in the now and turn his bed around so he could enjoy the garden, the humming birds and the bees. I listened and reassured him that life was an eternal gift and that God had given us this human experience to find the opportunity to live in peace and embrace love. Every moment contains gifts and opportunities that are invisible to the untrained mind. It is easy to get lost. Death is the wakeup call that signals us to stop living in the future and start living in the now.

I had another client diagnosed with ALS (Lou Gehrig's Disease) who was a very good friend with my wife. She was told she had two years to live. Every Monday my wife would visit her and they would laugh and cry and talk. Gradually she lost her ability to walk, eat and speak, but she never lost her ability to love. Love was her specialty. She was a student of the principle of love and was prepared for life's transformation. She was always more interested in you than she was in herself or her condition. She lived for six years, and when she died, my wife laid on the bed next to her and sang Irish lullabies as she peacefully passed away.

We are gifted just so many breaths, and each breath is another opportunity to live in love's peace of mind. Where will you be mentally when you take that last breath? Most are overly concerned with location and not prepared for where they will be *mentally* when transformation becomes reality. It's not the physical that matters as much as the sacred.

*"To the well-organized mind,
death is but the next great adventure."*
—J. K. Rowling
Harry Potter and the Sorcerer's Stone

Chapter 2
The Fear of Death or The Fear of Life

The context of your belief is the key

Fear is both challenge and opportunity because it signals our minds that a change is trying to emerge. I am surprised by how many signals I ignore and how many signs I miss. There will always be that part of me that says, "I should have seen that coming."

Our worldview is a reflex that automatically focuses on conditions and circumstances and has no time scheduled for the disruption of death. This part of our lives takes a direct hit when we encounter death. After all, who has death scheduled on their calendar?

The initial reaction is an attempt to attach meaning to something that defies meaning. It stirs a deep sense of fear and relief, an odd combination that reminds us of our mortal nature and lack of control over something we're all going to have to face. If it's somebody close—a partner, spouse, brother, sister, mother, father, or relative—death can be a *game changer*. When the loss of a trusted confidante, provider, a source of love, income and stability is not there, it changes everything. This is even more upsetting when you lose several loved ones over a brief period of time. It is a wake-up call that brings up a great deal of uncertainty and doubt—not about death, but about life!

The fear of life is not uncommon. It is the cause of much of our indecision and hesitation. Most people are not guided by their passion; they're guided by their fear. For example, people will stay in a profession they hate because they're afraid of being unemployed; or they will stay in an unhealthy relationship because they fear loneliness; or they will do everything they can to stay alive because they fear death. Death is the catalyst that brings these feelings to the surface and mixes them in an emotional gumbo that is hard to swallow and

The Fear of Death or the Fear of Life

doesn't sit well in our gut. For most, death is unwelcome news. This message is disturbing because we spend too much time feeling afraid, lost in the *why,* with life's lessons half learned or worse, misinformed by the opinions of those equally confused. Then death knocks on our door, and we hear the clock ticking.

Some profess they have no fear of death, yet they do not trust the life they have been given to live. What is the fear that drives so many to distrust life? Some engage only a small portion of life's potential. They live just enough to keep themselves secure and safe, beyond which they're too afraid to venture. That point, however, is breached when death wakes us up and demands that we look at what we're afraid of. But we have clever egos that shut off the wakeup call, convincing us that we're too busy to deal with our emotional distrust.

Eventually we grieve, and if we're willing, we will learn the purpose of death and transformation. If we are prepared, our death, or the death of loved one, reminds us to look at the *big picture* and see the opportunities life provides. If we are unprepared, the unforgiven mistakes, the unresolved resentments, the second guessing, and the unfulfilled desires come to the surface like the bones of dinosaurs rising out of some ancient tar pit. These are the things we hold suspended in our subconscious minds, ready to run wild and destroy our confidence at the first sign of fear. We must dismiss it all for what it is, "False Evidence Appearing Real." "False" because we believe our limitations to be true and our conditions insurmountable. "Real" because we see only what we believe, and we have trained our minds to engage life as a problem thus, we see our problems as permanent fixtures that must be solved before we can feel alive. This is a puzzle we force ourselves to solve over and over until we see the insanity of this way of living. Thus, the meaning of that old idea, *insanity is doing the same thing over and over expecting a different result,* or *solving the same problem over and over expecting a different answer.*

I've seen people become confused and distracted by these dinosaurs—the monsters of memory suspended in fear and used by our egos to create expectations and distort our ability to imagine a greater life. There is one miracle, however, that is a remedy to such a distorted life—Love!

The one thing—and according to some, the only thing we will be judged by—is *how much did we love each other*. Love can cast out our fear when it defines our reason for being alive. The fear of death and life disappear when love lights the way. As one spiritual philosopher put it, "And the light shineth in the darkness; and the darkness comprehended it not."

When love dismantles our fear, our old lives give way to a new life, a life lived in a sacred framework—informed, inspired, and intentional.

You do not have to compromise

Most people are perplexed by death. For many, it feels like a compromise, or worse, a failure, or for some, a chance to escape the mindlessness of existence. Life was never created for escape. It was created so we might know the nature of *eternity* and the blessings of *unlimited good.* Life provides us the opportunity to see ourselves in relation to others and apply the power of love and forgiveness. This is the power of a prepared mind. As one great thinker put it, "The resurrection is the *death of the belief* that we are separated from God."

Many see death as an illusion created by humanity to explain their exit. After all, you can't die without a reason. If you do, they have to do an autopsy. This is especially true in Western cultures. Life, however, is an eternal reality. God does not die. Once we understand the power of love and how to use it, we wake up to life and begin to live with purpose. Rather than feeling alone, isolated or unfulfilled we engage life in every conversation and transaction. We refuse to compromise. We refuse to live in fear. We insist that love is the answer and that peace is the way.

This is the awakening that humanity is seeking. To know this, you would have to accept a new *contextual perception* (a frame of mind) that a great good lives within each of us, that this good is seeking our attention, waiting upon our resurrection (our reconnection with God). Is it possible? The challenge is how we make sense of this concept and integrate it into our worldview so we can free ourselves from fear. The way to do this is simple.

Instead of our time spent in fear, we teach ourselves to live in love, not compromised by our disbeliefs and over-invested in the negative—stumbling, lost, and pretending that it doesn't matter. No one can live a life of love in a negative state of mind. The truth is, when we live in the faith *of* God and not the faith in God, our faith becomes a passion for life. Death is no longer an issue and fear is no longer allowed to stand in our way. This is the opposite of a life lived in a fear that yells in our heads, "Survive, don't Live."

Do you think I have overstated fear? Do you live with a lot of concerns and worry? This way of life is not always obvious and it rarely rises into our awareness unless threatened by a catastrophic event, like a death in the family.

Fear is a collective phenomenon buried deep in the *subconscious,* lurking within, waiting to be summoned by Death's call to action. If you were prepared and death disrupted your life, you could choose to let love call you out. You could choose to make no more excuses for withholding love and failing to live in peace.

The death of a loved one or a personal expiration date will call you out into the open and give you another opportunity to become the agent of love or the agent of fear. Which will you choose?

If love prevails, old wounds will heal; family members reunite and children see their divorced parents quietly talking, forgiving, and accepting life's changes. I've seen the power of love take hold at memorials that I've officiated, especially at the end of my memorial message when I tell those in attendance, "I know some of you have big holes in your heart, the hole was put there by the love of the *dearly departed* who you're missing. The best way to honor your missing loved one is to fill that hole *by loving others the way they loved you.* Break the ice and turn life into a fluid experience of goodness, patience and love."

Honoring the process of what you believe

Death is an opportunity to clear the air about what we believe. It is a cosmic shove in the direction of who we think we are. Here is the truth, EVERYONE DIES AND EVERYONE LIVES FOREVER. How can this be?

Eternity is an endless experience of *form* following *function*. This is an old interior-design saying and it makes sense because why would anyone want furniture that looked good but was uncomfortable? Or, to explain the metaphor, why would you strive to create a life that looked good but was hard to live in and a struggle to maintain? If you think the function of your life is to maintain an image and sustain a life of wealth, stature, and power you will burn-out, die, and wonder What was the purpose?

A number of years ago I met a woman, Grace Bubulka, who had a *near-death experience* that had been written up in the 1960s in Life magazine. Grace had written a book and was giving presentations on her experience. She described what I had read in much of my research, a movement toward the light and a meeting with a figure she identified as Jesus. This was accompanied with an overwhelming feeling of *being loved*. She then spoke of a life-review, not a review of everything in your life, only the parts where you had the opportunity to love. I wondered if Grace was satisfied. Had she done a good job? Could she have done better?

Then, Eureka! Could I have done better? Could I do better? Suddenly, lifted to a whole new way of seeing, I began to feel the power of love and the reason for my existence. This was a pivotal experience. It turned me towards love and made *my fear* disappear. Death was not a reality in Spirit; it was a misunderstanding that had little bearing on who I was or why I was. My eternality was already the truth and that truth was setting me free to love on a completely different frequency, a frequency that was a new signal to the world that I was here to give meaning to love and I was no longer *dying to live*.

"The function of prayer is not to influence God, but rather to change the nature of the one who prays."
—**Søren Kierkegaard**

Chapter 3
Prayers

Peace of Mind

Life is not a one-trick pony. The process of death, when it is not aimed at peace of mind, defaults to fear. Life is dimensional and it must be respected in all its dimensions. Those who ignore the process of life by not being proactive and procreative will default to the process of death by *fear*; and that will look like the only *doorway* out of this experience. Life is a conscious choice and it is a choice we must make each day. The benefit of this choice is peace of mind—or as some might describe it, the Peace of God and *knowing* that life is an eternal experience. The choice, however, is not automatic. It must, by necessity, be made by each person each day. This is not an option, it is a requirement.

Prayer is a choice. It is a conscious decision to write, speak and contemplate a specific idea about what one desires and what one is willing to stop thinking and start thinking. In my tradition, prayer begins by recognizing God as the one substance of life. The Divine is a Universal Intelligence that can be shaped into a particular experience through the conscious sum of ones thoughts, feelings, and emotions. As human beings, our primary function is to think, feel, and then react. Our reactions are almost all driven by our emotions, not our feelings. For the purpose of this book, let me state that I define a difference between how you feel and how you emotionally react.

Emotions, in my book, are memorized reactions, a conditioned reflex. Feelings are the pure and unfettered responses of the Divine, e.g., unconditional love versus conditional acceptance based on how you behave. When I use love as a *defining mechanism,* it clarifies my behavior and governs and edits my words. When I use fear or any other memorized reactions as my *defining mechanism* it confounds and frustrates me, distorting what I think and feel. This is what leads to depression and unhappiness.

On the other hand, if I consciously use love to define my behavior, I can succeed. Even if the slings and arrows of outrageous fortune are flung in my direction, I let them pass and live in peace. This is the power of love. This is what I pray upon and focus my conscious mind on.

What needs to be healed?

If you are in the process of death and you are willing to pass, should people be praying for you to get better? If you die, is your healing a failure? What needs to be healed is mostly about ones separation from their *higher power*.

This is the place in this book where the reader must decide to live in eternal oneness with God or see themselves separate and isolated. The intellect, when it becomes a tool of the ego, can only see separation. It cannot reconcile itself as one with God. Even if you believe in a God that is separate from you, your ego will insist that you're on your own and that you must take responsibility for your life. This means you must also take responsibility for your death. This leads to a strange anomaly that says you cannot die unless you have a good reason.

If you believe in your complete and absolute connection with God and God and you are one, you can't die. You can only transform (change) and transcend (go beyond). Yes, you will leave the physical body and rise out of the *human condition*. You will pass into a new form, and your awareness of who you are will go with you. Death is not failure. It is a cosmic shove into a new form and greater potential for peace, love, beauty and joy. Life is not a condition. Life is an infinite journey of spiritual growth and cosmic understanding.

There is nothing wrong about wanting to stay in the human condition. It is a very addictive experience and if you are adept at living you will probably not want to leave. Change, however, is inevitable and eventually you will transform and go beyond the human condition. What needs to be healed is any fear about this process and a willingness to understand that change is not death. It is a means by which we grow and are given the opportunity to be an even greater expression of—dare I say it—love.

Prayers that light the way, deepen your faith, take away the fear, and focus you on peace

Can prayer light the way and deepen your faith? It can if you know how to pray. Prayer, in most religions, is a pleading to a power outside of us for a change in outcome. In my spiritual tradition, what you pray for is not as important as how you pray.

Prayer in my tradition is not about begging or pleading; it is about belief in the oneness of life, faith in the ability of life to respond to my word, and the acceptance of life as an infinite experience filled with a greater and greater feeling of love. My tradition sees prayer as an opportunity to open an avenue of healing within. Prayer shapes my experience with statements that recognize God as the one and only power and substance of life. As I unify with this Divine and Universal Presence and declare the truth about what life is and how it functions within, I see myself operating as its agent.

In the following examples the first statement I make is recognizing God as the one power and presence of life. Then I unify with that idea and declare my life as one with God's Life. Then I speak my word for whatever I want to demonstrate in my life.

Example 1: God is the Power and Presence. God's love is universal and creative. I stand in unity with God's presence and know that It is the Creative Intelligence that created me. Right now, I declare God's Power and Presence to be my power and presence and I speak my word for a prosperous, loving, and peaceful life. In this moment, God's Love functions as my love, unconditional, forever emerging as my compassion, fulfilling all that I desire in truth. AND SO IT IS!

Example 2: God's Peace is everywhere. God's Intelligence is in all. I am God's Peace and every part of my life functions as that Peace in all that I say, do, and serve. In this moment, God's Peace takes away any doubt or uncertainty and opens my heart to a greater love and a greater peace. Filled with God's Grace, my feelings of gratitude know no bound. I am the active and physical presence of Peace, Love and Joy. AND SO IT IS!

Now let's add two more steps to this method, Gratitude and Release. The following is a five-step prayer specifically written to *Light the Way*.

Recognition: God is Light. God understands. God knows how to express by means of Its creation.

Unity: I am God's Light functioning by means of what I understand. I am now one with a greater understanding that propels my sense of confidence and faith.

Declaration: Right now, I function as that which illumines life and brings love. Every part of my being and my experience reveals a deep and abiding connection to a greater and greater Truth. I am the functional presence of a great Light that dispenses the uncertainty and darkness of all and any thoughts that would cast a shadow upon my life.

Gratitude: I am thankful for all my blessings and even the negative experiences that help to strengthen my resolve to live in peace. There is so much to be grateful for.

Release: I let go and accept that God's Power now takes hold of my word. As I release it into the Creative Intelligence, my word is grasped by the Universal and my experience is now manifested.

Example 3: A five-step prayer to **Deepen Your Faith**

God's Faith is the reality of life. God believes in creation and is eternally creating out of Its own Faith. God is the creator of all life.

My life is God's Life functioning in my Faith of God. Because I am the creative outcome of God's Divine Intelligence, I trust the life I have been given to live. Every part of my life is the outcome of God's Faith and Creative Genius.

In this moment, I go deeper in my Love of God and higher in my Love of Life. Every moment is a divine gift animated by God's complete faith in my creation. Every day is a revelation that helps me advance my sense of Peace, Prosperity, and Joy.

Today, God's Love is my guide to a greater experience of Peace. Today, God's faith is my faith.

Thank you, God, for all the goodness of who I am. I am grateful for every moment, condition, person, and opportunity you provide.

Released, my word is the truth and the law from which I stem. All is released into God's Faith and all is returned as my perfect experience.

Example 4: A five-step prayer to **Take Away the Fear** (each step indicated.)

Recognition: God is the whole, perfect and complete idea of living. God's presence is my presence.

Unify: I am the whole, perfect and complete idea of God. I am one with God's Presence because I am the individualized idea of God's Presence.

Declare: Today, I am the whole, perfect, and complete idea of Love in action. Every moment is yet another opportunity to practice Love. My love casts out all my uncertainty. I cannot live in fear and love simultaneously. Each day is a choice and I chose Love. There is no other place I live and find peace than Love

Gratitude: I am so grateful for God's Love. I accept the unconditional nature in which God moves through me, for me, as me bringing all the good I experience.

Release: It is my pleasure to release my word into God's Perfect Presence and Power knowing that God is the Source and Supply of everything I experience. I accept the fulfillment of this Word as an immediate action. AND SO IT IS!

"For every minute you remain angry, you give up sixty seconds of peace of mind."
—**Ralph Waldo Emerson**

Chapter 4
Family and Friends

Have no expectation

When people have expectations and life doesn't meet those expectations, it can be cause to a lot of disappointment and limitation. It is useful to understand the nature of expectations and how they affect your life when you receive your expiration notice. Every person in your family and circle of friends will have a different response to your news. How you choose to give them the news will have a definite influence upon how they process their feelings.

Time to Leave

There is no way to predict how anyone will react to the news of your expiration. All will be different. Death is a catalyst for change. It forces everyone to look at their preconceived ideas about life, purpose, meaning and eternality. Depending on how a person has woven their way into your heart will determine the depth of grief and the kinds of changes they will experience.

What everyone has in common is the need to *process* their sense of loss and how it will redefine the way they live in the world. You, the soon to be expired, may not grasp this immediately because you will be *processing* your own feelings, and for a while that process will be all-consuming. It will take time, but it can be useful to consider how you choose to share the news. The more you express peace and confidence in your transition, the more likely you will help your friends and family be at ease with your passing.

This is not possible in all cases. Many times such news is given to everyone simultaneously. This could happen at an emergency room, the scene of an accident, or a phone call. This is one of the reasons I am writing this book.

Part of the intended emphasis of this book is to be prepared. Preparation, however, is not spelled *s-t-u-d-y*.

Family and Friends

Preparation is *practice*. It is a constant application of key ideas that condition the way we think and behave.

Take time each day to consider, in your thoughts and activities, the practice of these five key points about life:

1. Never take the people you love for granted. Tell all you love that you're grateful for their presence in your life.
2. Take time each day to give thanks for all your blessings and consciously bless all the people you have had the privilege to know.
3. From time to time, conspire to express your gratitude in loving and thoughtful ways. Who would not be moved by an unexpected card or a note of gratitude?
4. Daily strengthen your relationship with God. Learn to pray every day for peace, patience and love and go to your place of worship to remind yourself who you are and how much you are loved.
5. Forgive yourself and all who need your forgiveness. Do not leave this world in hatred, fear or doubt. Whatever mindset you come from, whether it's love, anger, peace, or confusion, that is where you're going to.

Take a 4 x 6 card and copy these ideas. Read them several times a day and put them to use each time you read. This is the practice. Each time you practice you will expand your capacity for love. Irrespective of conditions, personalities, or circumstances you can change the way you think and live. Practice, prepare, and rise. The opportunity for redemption is offered in every moment with every breath.

Patience, Compassion, and Love

When a loved one is dying some family and friends struggle with *what* to say or *how* to act. The struggle we have with the idea of death is symptomatic of where we have failed to prepare. I know of very few people who have a well-developed sense of what life and death are or how they choose to think of them.

Most of what we know about life and death is drawn from what we have observed, read, or heard. But it wasn't that way in the past. Before the onset of mass media, death was a very personal and frequent experience. Before the advance of medicine almost everyone was forced to deal with death very early on. No one was excused from some direct and sudden passing of a family member or friend. Famine, plagues, disasters, and accidents of all kinds were far more frequent and devastating. Up until the last century infant mortality was common and lifespans were much shorter.

While we may lack the direct experience of our ancestors, death still stimulates our memories and floods us with feelings of helplessness. We may lack the coping skills our ancestors had to develop, but we still share the shock and despair death requires us to process.

When it comes to death, we put off growing up and defer emotional maturation. Western culture has figured out how to bury its feelings. The collective desire to live a long life is a powerful motivator that pushes the idea of death deeper into the subconscious. Who wants to deal with it until you have to?

For those who choose to develop their feelings about death and prepare themselves for that inevitable experience, there are a number of spiritual skills that will serve you well: patience, compassion and love.

Patience is derived from an old Latin word, *impertubalilis,* which means not to be disturbed or made anxious. This is an art developed by staying centered on a Principle and not a condition. A Principle is a *defining mechanism,* which means that a Principle instructs and inspires a very specific form of behavior. A condition, circumstance or personality rarely instructs. It causes one to react without thinking. It forces us into memorized patterns of emotional rejection, judgment, limitation, and inflexibility.

Time to Leave

Principles create opportunities to see life from a different angle. They become a cause for change because Principles compel us to *think different thoughts,* in spite of how we want to react. A Principle is a reminder that we are not just dealing with the world and all that it demands. We are dealing with a Universal Truth and all that it is ready to provide the moment we use the Principle to shape and define our behavior.

For instance, many times, as a minister, I am called to visit a congregant in the hospital. On the way to see the patient, I work on the Principle of Compassion to prepare my mind for what I might see, hear or have to respond to. Whether it is a serious diagnosis that has put an expiration notice into play or an accident that has created some doubt of well-being, I work from the Principle and not the condition. What that means is I am always working from Love and God's ever present capacity to heal and bring peace to every condition, circumstance, and person.

The Principle, once it becomes my reason for being there, changes how I see things unfolding and what people need. For many, it is just to be with them while they process their feelings. For others, it is a conversation that reassures them that there is a higher power functioning within and that peace is a choice they can make. It is the power of Love that casts out fear and causes all to feel God's love moving within, calming their hearts and comforting their minds. This is the way patience, compassion and love works to heal and create the necessary awareness that takes almost everyone to a place of faith and trust. Inescapably, patience, love and peace are always a choice.

A number of years ago a friend of mine had gone to the dentist for a toothache and found out he had cancer on the left side of his face. In less than 48 hours he was in the hospital and the entire front of his face had been lifted off to remove his right eye, eye brow, and cheek bone. The doctors then reattached his face and when I got to the hospital he had just come out of surgery and was conscious. I walked into the recovery room and he was sitting up. His face was stitched back into place with drainage tubes coming out of all sides, and a huge bandage where his right eye had been removed. I immediately started in with prayer reaffirming my ability to be of loving support and to look past the visible to the complete healing of his face. He acknowledged my presence by writing on a tablet some form of humor, which I can't remember, but it was a clear indication that he was using all that he knew to stay present to his healing and focused on being alive.

Time to Leave

This is what I mean about being prepared and able to use the knowledge you have developed about the eternal to handle the circumstances you sometimes encounter.

I focused on engaging God's patience, love and compassion. As a team of nurses helped him through this experience, I wrote and said aloud at least three prayers. These prayers were not only to heal him but to heal my mind that he was in mortal danger. If you are going to know the truth about life, you must learn to cast out the fear and remember that there is no death!

My friend lived several more years. Not easy years…years of struggle. The same kind of struggle witnessed in the life of the caterpillar. Transformed by an internal signal, layer upon layer builds within the chrysalis and the caterpillar is changed into a butterfly. It then emerges in a mighty struggle that is necessary to strengthen its wings. Without the struggle the butterfly could not fly.

The moral of this story is, no matter how much we would like to believe we are in control, we are not! You cannot control death, but you can shape a frame of mind and resolve yourself to live in a new form.

The logic of the Infinite is change, constant and relentless change. This is an undisputed truth that renders all form *incapable of eternal status*. Even the human form will disappear because it is ill-equipped to live eternally. Look within, however, and you will find an *eternal Spirit* individualized as your life. It is our spirit that is equipped to live eternally and transform from one form to a new form. This is what my friend was experiencing, shaping the last few years of his life into a meaningful existence that helped him transform and learn to love.

Many are afraid of the struggle and pain it seems to cause. For this reason a whole science of how to control our symptoms has emerged: Palliative Care.

Hospice

What is Hospice? How does Hospice change the medical approach to the patient? Why is Hospice valuable?

Hospice is an approach that focuses on, "quality, compassionate care for people facing a life-limiting illness or injury. Hospice care involves a team-oriented approach to expert medical care, pain management, and emotional and spiritual support expressly tailored to the patient's needs and wishes. Support is provided to the patient's loved ones as well."

How does hospice change the medical approach to the patient? Once admitted to a Hospice program, the medical decisions on the care of the patient are built around the diagnosis that there is no cure, and that the primary care for the patient is to provide all necessary treatment to relieve pain and tailor the care to the patient's needs and wishes. There is also support for the family provided by a team of nurses, social workers, clergy, counselors, trained volunteers and physical therapists as needed.

Why is Hospice valuable? Hospice is an approach to the experience of death that keeps maturing and growing. Hospice is a powerful movement that has profoundly changed the way we die. Millions of people now regularly die with dignity, surrounded by loved ones, family and friends. And even though it has grown in popularity, the services of Hospice do not start until the patient has received the diagnosis.

Don't wait until you need Hospice. Make a conscious choice to educate yourself about death and make the important decisions before those decisions are forced upon a loved one that is not prepared to make the choices that would best serve you.

More information can be found online by searching the word Hospice on Google.

Palliative Care

"Palliative care (pronounced pal-lee-uh-tiv) is specialized medical care for people with serious illnesses. It focuses on providing patients with relief from the symptoms, pain, and stress of a serious illness—whatever the diagnosis. The goal is to improve quality of life for both the patient and the family.

Palliative care is provided by a team of doctors, nurses and other specialists who work together with a patient's other doctors to provide an extra layer of support. It is appropriate at any age and at any stage in a serious illness and can be provided along with curative treatment.

The Quality of Life

Palliative care treats people suffering from serious and chronic illnesses such as cancer, cardiac disease such as congestive heart failure (CHF), chronic obstructive pulmonary disease (COPD), kidney failure, Alzheimer's, Parkinson's, Amyotrophic Lateral Sclerosis (ALS) and many more.

Palliative care focuses on symptoms such as pain, shortness of breath, fatigue, constipation, nausea, loss of appetite, difficulty sleeping, and depression. It also helps you gain the strength to carry on with daily life. It improves your ability to tolerate medical treatments. It helps you have more control over your care by improving communication so that you can better understand your choices for treatment."

http://www.getpalliativecare.org

If you have any kind of serious or chronic illness that you think would be causing you pain and discomfort in the future, you should ask for a physician that specializes in Palliative care. A proactive approach is necessary to learn the protocols you might experience as your conditions changes. Since there are differences in how doctors who specialize in Palliative care approach pain and discomfort, it would be helpful to research and get recommendations from other physicians and people you know.

"Whenever you read a cancer booklet or website or whatever, they always list depression among the side effects of cancer. But, in fact, depression is not a side effect of cancer. Depression is a side effect of dying."
—**John Green**
The Fault in Our Stars

Chapter 5
What to Say and How to Listen

Listen first then what to share

Conversations, coma, consciousness, and being alive: It's a challenge to figure out what to say to a person who's been given an expiration date. What is there to talk about: The diagnosis, emotions, feelings, family, arrangements and treatment? If you've had no experience with this conversation, it can feel confusing and uncertain. It's normal to wonder if you are doing this right.

What to ask when you don't know the person or much about their history or condition

The first question I ask: What do you know about your condition? This gives the patient an opportunity to share their story—the narrative of what has happened. It's important that you listen, nod you head, be receptive…stay quiet. Encourage the person to tell you as much as they can remember. Sometimes that means staying quiet while they think about what they want to say. Listening builds a cognitive connection. The patient feels heard. The more they talk, the more they connect. If you interrupt this process, it limits the patient's sense of connection and the listener's ability to serve.

If the patient feels cut off or not heard, they can withdraw, feeling isolated and unsupported. Listening takes energy and concentration. You must pay attention with lots of eye contact and, through your facial expressions, indicate that you're listening.

After the patient has fully expressed, it is appropriate to say that you're sorry they have to go through this and that this is an unavoidable experience.

What to Say and How to Listen

This might seem obvious but confirming this is your way of saying, "I hear you." Other questions could include anything you didn't understand: the time-frame the doctor has put on you, or are you going to stay in the hospital or go home? Whatever you think needs more clarity, ask. But don't push. If the patient can't answer, shift the conversation to people who need to know: family, friends, minister, and business associates. Ask if the patient needs help making phone calls. Then after everything about their condition has been discussed, talk about the future and the stuff you share in common. This confirms that they are still alive, that there are things to talk about, and that their opinions matter. Talking about life when they're spiritually centered helps them focus on being confident and integrated, not isolated. This conversation emphasizes the reality of who they are, not what they're going through. Even if they are going to leave the human condition soon, prayer, forgiveness, and affirmations are still essential to practicing peace of mind.

Unconscious or in a coma, there is still a chance the patient can hear you. Dying does not mean the patient is deaf. Even in a coma-like state, even if they are termed "brain dead," I believe people still hear you.

Time to Leave

Recently I was with 12 people in an intensive care room all saying good bye to a beautiful friend. The nurse unhooked the life support, and in less than a minute the person stopped breathing, turned ashen gray and left the body. Even as the person died, many of her family and friends continued to wish her well, reassuring her that she was loved.

Death is a point of departure. It is the place where we wait for that moment when called out of the *human condition* we transcend and re-form ourselves into the *spiritual experience.* As on earth, the spiritual experience must be in-line with ones spiritual beliefs. Just like you can't plant corn and expect to get tomatoes, you can't be of one belief and as you transcend not become the experience of that belief. If you're Christian, I have no doubt you will meet Jesus. If you are Jewish, I have no doubt you will meet Moses and maybe even Joshua. If you're Buddhist, you will be given the opportunity to break whatever cycle of life you are experiencing over and over and enter a new era of life that transcends the necessity to reincarnate. All religions offer a path to God, and all religions have an idea of who you are and what you are becoming. I am not the arbiter of such beliefs. I honor the beliefs of people even if I don't share them. I honor them because this is their death and they need to process it according to their own beliefs.

Since I believe all will transcend into their own experience according to what they believe, my job is to make sure they know they are loved and that life is eternal.

Conversations with older folks

Recently I was visiting a member of our center in her late 80s and was in a hospital because of an obstruction in her bowls. It took two days to clear her system and she was exhausted. When I got to her, she was trying to get her strength up to go home. Her daughter said that she had almost died that morning and no one was sure if she was going to be well enough to travel. I sat down next to her bed and touched her arm and called her name. She opened her eyes. They had positioned a clear plastic mask on her face that covered her nose and mouth and was held in place by an adjustable strap. She tried to talk but the mask made it impossible. Her son reached over and touched the call button for the nurse, and soon the rehab specialist stuck his head into the room and asked if we needed something.

It took just a few moments to remove the mask and put those smaller nubs attached to a light oxygen line in her nose with the line around her ears. Much more comfortable, she looked into my eyes, focused and smiled. She recognized me and the conversation started. There was no need to discuss her condition. Her daughter gave me all the information, and the one thing she wanted to do was go home.

I could see she was afraid. I knew that she loved flowers, and I asked her what her favorite flower was.

"Roses," she replied.

"Aren't they wonderful?" I responded. She nodded and smiled. We talked a little bit more about roses and then I asked her if she had any other favorite flowers.

"Gardenias," she said.

"Yes, I like those too. I remember my mother loved the smell of those flowers and would cut the blooms and then float them in a bowl of water." We talked about flowers and her daughter's talent to create such beautiful gardens.

The point of all this was to engage her in a conversation that calmed her and gave her a chance to regain some sense of being *okay*. We talked for over 45 minutes and her doctor came in the room and wanted to listen to her heart. I exited with the daughter and *suggested* that she get her home as soon as possible.

Later the next day, she did just that, went home. The caregivers and hospice were there to greet her but it didn't go smooth. She was upset with the oxygen mask they wanted her to wear, and although she was home, she began to panic and started to remove the mask and her clothing. The nurse on call gave her a larger dose of morphine and that quieted her mood.

When I asked about liquids and food, her daughter confirmed that she desired neither. This is normal. The mother was home for two days and then passed peacefully in her sleep.

When a person is starting to move toward their transition, it is typical to stop taking water and refuse to eat. Then they begin to sleep more, and with the medication to keep them calm, they will go into a sort of coma-like state. From time to time they will wake up and ask where they are and maybe want some ice to relieve the dry mouth caused by breathing through their mouth. Eventually, though, they stop waking up and the body begins to shut down. The lungs begin to fill with fluid and it doesn't take long before the heart stops and they leave this earthly plane bound for the *other side.*

This is how I have observed many people pass, but it is not always this way. Some folks will struggle with breathing and others will last for several days longer than they're supposed too, perhaps waiting for a loved one to stop by and bid them farewell. Everyone is different and there is no way to say exactly how each will accomplish their passing. The most important thing is to stay the watch and know the truth—that life is eternal and they are loved.

Family Dynamics

When my father passed, my brother, sister, and I were all standing watch at hospital. Dad was blocked and was beginning to experience uremic poisoning. But he wasn't giving up. It was morning and I had to go to my office and take care of a few calls. My brother was with him and said go ahead, I will watch. On my way back to hospital my bother called and said the train had left the station (this was code for Dad had passed).

My sister and I arrived at the same time and the three of us stood next to dad's bed, held hands and said goodbye. We all cried and promised to take care of each other, and we have. That night my wife made us dinner and we ate and told stories of our youth. Such is the miracle of loving families who appreciate their parents.

Not all, of course, have had good memories about their parents; and this is where *forgiveness* is so important. My wife Patty, was estranged from her father for years and had witnessed him abuse her mother. We talked about the importance of forgiveness and how those who don't forgive tend to hang on to resentments and anger—that those memories can cause all kinds of internal strife and unhappiness.

She worked with a prayer partner and began to forgive her dad and was working up the courage to call him when he called her. His son, my wife's half-brother, was getting married and he wanted her to come to the wedding. These are the miracles that happen when your intention is forgiveness.

Finding balance and peace of mind in the process of grief

Grief and sorrow are two mountains, which once climbed, offer an unexpected view. To climb those mountains requires balance and peace of mind. Like any climb, the angle can be challenging and it requires endurance. If you are overly invested in the pain of separation, feeling isolated and alone, the climb will go slow. If you are vested in a deeper sense of peace and you've practiced being peaceful, you can accelerate and move quickly to a sense of acceptance and balance.

The example of this is the horrific experience of losing a child. There is no pain I can think of that compares. Children are our investment in the future and nobody is ready to lose a child. In my experience working with parents who've lost children it takes a while but the parents, in most cases, will get close to God and begin to experience a deep and abiding peace. It is possible to feel loss and simultaneously be at peace. One of the most important attributes of humanity is the ability to think one thing and feel another.

Many years ago, when I was first a minister, a family came to me who had suffered the loss of a teenage son. His death was an accident, and we made an appointment to discuss his memorial. At the same time I was working with a congregant who was painting angels. She was working on a series of angels from different traditions. Her first painting was that of a young adolescent boy with wings and a halo. She had just completed the painting and hung the picture in the sanctuary. When the parents walked in, the mother, who was overwhelmed with emotion, saw the painting and froze. The father was equally transfixed. Both parents shared that the picture was the exact likeness of their son when he was a little boy.

As we sat down to discuss the memorial their demeanor dramatically changed, the exact opposite of what I had observed the day before. Their anguish and pain disappeared. They were peaceful. I have observed this on other occasions, and even though I am familiar with this phenomenon, I am still surprised at how fast people's attitude can change. Peace is contagious. It is the grace of God readjusting the inner sense of being and bringing an inner calm that allows one to regain a sense of poise and balance.

Grief is a spiritual experience and a healing wonder. It is as if the hand of God reaches into our hearts and peacefully calms our emotional stress and rearranges our inner sense of identity. It heals the cavity created by loss and renders us well in spite of our feelings of separation. Not all, however, experience the healing right away. Some have what Dr. David Burns, the author of *Feeling Good*, calls a *distorted* sense of reality that makes the feeling of loss unfair and unnatural. The conclusion is they have been robbed and cheated of a relationship which could never be replaced, that they will never be the same, and they will never recover their sense of balance or peace.

Too many people put their lives on hold because of unresolved loss. Many will self-medicate and some will simply withdraw. Much of this can be mitigated if you take a little time to reflect upon the temporary nature of being human. Life is short, maybe 80 to 90 years, but being alive and able to interact with others is one of the greatest miracles ever created. Once we shed our sense of insecurity and our collective fear of loss, we will embrace life with gratitude and replace our uncertainty with trust and our fear with love.

On average, it takes a person about 45 to 60 days to heal from the loss of a loved one. Gradually they readjust and engage life with a new sense of enthusiasm. I am not sure how long it takes for the dearly departed to adjust. By all account,s it depends on how prepared you are to move on. For those who have punctured the veil of infinite life and returned to report their experience, their observations are encouraging and inspire a great sense of optimism. It would appear that on the *other side* there is a new and exciting experience of freedom, peace and love. A love that is so intense, that many who have returned can't wait to get back.

On seeing dead people

When I first started to investigate life after death experiences, there was little mention of people seeing dead family members before they died. My first recollection of this was when my Aunt Ruth passed away in the mid-1960s and was reported to be talking to her deceased brother Chuck shortly before her death. The conclusion in the family was the poor woman was just going crazy.

Since then, it seems far more widespread that people conjure up past relatives who appear to them just before they die.

The older woman, whom I spoke with about flowers, was reported to be talking with her deceased brother just before she went to the hospital. Her caregiver had overheard the conversation, and when she was told there was no one in the room, she asked, "Well, then, who were all those other people in the room?"

Indeed, if there is no death and we meet our past relatives on the other side, why would it be unusual if we could see them before we crossed over?

If you believe, as I do, in the ongoing continuity of life, it would seem to dictate an ongoing identity and ability to communicate. So why not be met by our past relatives before we die?

It's easy to label people crazy for having this experience, and frequently that is the case, especially in Western medicine. I don't label this as crazy. I have had too many folks report this experience just before they died, and they died more peacefully knowing someone they knew was waiting to greet them.

The reason I say this is not to convince anyone that this is true but to make sure that you do not disagree with a friend or loved one in the process of dying who is having this experience. Maybe it's true and maybe it isn't true, but if it makes it easier for the person dying to move through their experience with more peace of mind, why not let them have that experience?

We are not here to argue the legitimate nature of what is occurring. We're here to listen, serve, and pray for their peaceful passing and loving experience.

Saying goodbye and the final curtain

The end is not the end. It is the beginning of a new chapter in spiritual evolution. No matter your religion or belief, no one is left behind. When you die and move behind the curtain, the revelation of how much you are loved, looked after and cared for is for many a surprise. My research and the many books I have read on death and dying reveal a consistency that life is an infinite experience, that death is a transition from the human condition of doubt and fear to the spiritual resurrection and the experience of love and peace.

So what about hell? Hell is a human invention based on fear and superstition. God did not create hell; humanity did. The collective memory of humanity has been absorbing death, torture, and loss and reimaging it until it appears as a shadow of fear that threatens our very existence. Exaggerated and amplified by our unwillingness to engage love, fear dominates the minds and souls of too many. It is our conscious memory filled with what we have heard, seen, smelled, tasted, and felt. It is the collective idea of what can go wrong in the human condition elevated to some religious place of rejection and damnation. This is not what the vast majority who die and return report. The mechanics of those who dwell in hell is the same for those who exaggerate the human experience through their imagination depicting and describing the human variables in life.

It is time to stop studying war and lay down our troubles…*down by the riverside*…to seek guidance from those wise and wonderful sages who instruct by example that life is a miracle, never to be taken for granted or minimized through shame or fear. We are the product of a Divine Intelligence that knows exactly what It created. We all have within us a seed of freedom ready to grow when we recognize Its Love as our redemption.

As one great philosopher put it, "The resurrection is the death of the belief that we are separated from God, for death is to the illusion alone and not to Reality. God did not die. What happened was that humanity woke up to Life. The awakening must be on the part of each person since God already is Life." The moment you grasp the reality of your Divine inheritance, you will return to your authority in the same way the prodigal son came home…he came to himself. "Our contention is not that dead people live again, *but that a living person never dies.*"

We no longer die to live. Instead we live and transcend the physical and recreate our presence in the spiritual nature of heaven. As one great spiritual teacher said, "There is no death, for God is not a God of the Dead but of the Living, and in God's eyes we are all alive and immortal."

Saying good bye is important, but I suggest you start by saying goodbye to every person you are leaving, even for a few hours, by seeing them in the light of love. Get into the habit of gratitude and grace and never allow yourself to hold on to any anger, resentment, and disappointment. Life is constantly changing, but love never changes. It is always present in the moment waiting upon our recognition, use and validation.

In some Buddhist traditions when a person experiences death, another person will read from the Tibetan Book of the Dead the instructions about how to break the cycles of reincarnation and move on to a higher experience of love and life. The assumption is that even though the body has died, the spirit is still present and can hear every word we say, and if they are listening, can be guided to a higher experience of life. No matter what you think about different religious traditions, they all seek to help the dead find their way to paradise or heaven. Such is the desire for all who are breaking the veil and passing into a whole new way of life.

Celebrate the passing of your loved ones and know that they did not die. Their spirits have reformed on the *other side* and they are still and will be forever creative beings of light, love and peace. And one day we will all be together. There is no death! Only eternal life!

"What you're supposed to do when you don't like a thing is change it. If you can't change it, change the way you think about it."
—**Maya Angelou**

Chapter 6
Passing Through: Stories of Transformation

The following are stories of transformation of people who were prepared for the experience and how that made all the difference.

Louis O.

Louis was 88 when I met him. I was the new minister of a small church in Cape Coral, Florida. Louis drew my attention because he always brought a different woman to church every Sunday. One day I

Time to Leave

asked Louis why he brought a different woman to church every Sunday. He pulled me aside and whispered that he had a colostomy bag and that he knew a lot of women who also had colostomy bags. He said many of them were too embarrassed to go out because they were afraid someone might notice, so he took these women out to help them gain confidence.

One morning after one of my Wednesday classes, Louis asked me for some prayer work because he was going to take his driver's test and he was concerned that he might not pass. He explained that he had just bought a new Oldsmobile and was looking forward to taking more of his friends out. I did the prayer work for him. He thanked me and left to pick up one of his lady friends to take them to lunch.

Around 2:30 p.m. I got a call from his friend. She said she had lunch with Louis and they walked outside and were standing on some grass next to Louis' new car. Halfway through their conversation, Louis looked at her and simply said, "I have to go." He then lay down on the grass and died. No struggle, no effort and no pain, Louis just died.

Later I was told that the coroner's office had picked up Louis and was required by law to do an autopsy because there was no apparent cause of death.

Passing Through: Stories of Transformation

I am sharing this story because Louis was prepared for life and transformation. Louis was always exploring spiritual paths that helped him understand the eternal and infinite nature of life. As a result, Louis became a student of living a life of oneness with God, and he applied this wisdom by allowing himself to be guided by his intuition. He believed in prayer and was devoted to helping others. He was also very successful in business. In fact, Louis was one of the first to open a series of Hospice Homes up and down the Eastern seaboard. He believed that everyone deserved to die in dignity surrounded by as much love as possible.

Louis was a good example of what happens when you practice a positive and affirmative approach to living.

In India it is a known fact that some spiritual leaders known as Yogis can leave this human condition by shutting down their metabolism and dying. This is difficult to understand in the Western world because hardly anyone in the West believes this is possible. Yet I have seen films of Yogis who have spent a lifetime practicing Yoga curl up into an extremely small box and shut down their metabolism to the point where they are just barely breathing yet still conscious. This form of meditation is called Samadhi. "Yogis are said to attain the final liberation or *videha mukti* after

leaving their bodies at the time of death. It is at this time that the soul knows a complete and unbroken union with the divine, and being free from the limitations of the body, merges effortlessly into the transcendent Self. Mahāsamādhi (literally *great samādhi*) is a term often used for this final absorption into the Self at death."
http://en.wikipedia.org/wiki/Samadhi

Dimensional prayer

In my spiritual practice I train people to use a form of meditation that I call *Dimensional Prayer*. This form of prayer will show you how to close the gap between you and God and help you stay aligned with the Divine. It uses controlled breathing and a series of hand motions known in Eastern traditions as Mudras. Just using the first step in Dimensional Prayer has great benefit in calming the mind and helping you become peaceful.

This practice involves consciously breathing, affirming and focusing your mind on the automatic ability of the body to breathe without you having to think. Observing this phenomenon will help some remember that they have a life and that life is breathing air into their experience in a consistent and automatic manner that animates their internal sense of being alive.

Life is an internal experience, and you can change your life by changing your thoughts. When you affirm that life is an eternal journey and that you are connected to God, the scope and range of your perception will begin to see endless opportunities to practice peace and express love. Love is an amazing phenomenon because you cannot be afraid as long as you are coming from love.

Love eliminates fear and brings an awareness of a deep and abiding power from which all of life stems. Once connected to this power through prayer, it is impossible to feel inadequate or incapable of peace.

This is what Louis knew to be the truth. He had a long and prosperous relationship with God, and he was keenly aware that his love and willingness to serve was the most important aspect of his life. People who learn this truth are not subject to the kinds of struggles that plague those of little faith. Even if they look like they're struggling, they are at ease because they see their struggle as a phase they are passing through on their way to a new life.

One way to develop your faith is to learn how to pray.

Learn to pray

The American Sign Language for God is to place the palm of the right hand perpendicular to your body and in front of your heart. Bring your hand to this position in a gentle sweeping motion while consciously inhaling and then exhaling. Hold the hand in position until all your air is expelled and then wait for God to take the next breath—don't try to hold your breath, just wait…your body will take it for you.

Try this exercise taking at least three normal breaths inhaling peace and exhaling love. Still your mind and God will reveal your inner intelligence.

When you combine this simple exercise with the conscious use of breath, it has a very calming effect. Doing these kinds of exercises can help focus your mind, especially if you are under a lot of stress. I know of people who have lowered their blood pressure using this practice. To learn the whole method you can go to www.JimTurrell.com and click on Learn to Pray.

Suzie V.

I'm not sure how long Suzie V. had been attending our Center. I was aware of her around 2006. She was a lively person who dressed to the nines and was well versed in what it meant to be one with God. Suzie and I were the same age; we both grew up in the '50 and '60s in Southern California. It wasn't until much later that I learned Suzie had leukemia but had refused chemotherapy opting for different medical and spiritual modalities. The one thing Suzie knew to do was to attend class and study the kinds of Principles that could help her stay focused on love in this part of her journey through the human condition.

Even though Suzie lived six years without traditional Western medicine, she knew that her body was not going to last forever. Suzie was interested in a holistic approach and prayed her way out of the fear that so often overwhelms those on this kind of journey.

I remember one of our last visits down on water's edge across the street from her Newport Beach home. Suzie loved the sun, and when I arrived, she was sitting outside at a picnic table. We sat and talked and I listened, observing her unstoppable courage. We talked about her family, her kids, and her father. I had the pleasure of knowing Suzie's father. He was a prayer practitioner at the Glendale church I attended in the early '70s; and, although, I never had any long talks with her dad, I observed and appreciated his dedication to serving others through prayer. Eventually, our conversation turned to her health and she talked about the worldwide connections she had made through Facebook. Suzie, it turns out, was loved by hundreds of people in many different countries around the world for her loving support and caring interest in others who were also struggling with a similar condition. She shared diets, medical modalities, and news with all her friends. She talked about how much they meant to her and how much fun she had in being that sort of *online Sage* from Newport Beach. As our conversation drew to a close, I did some prayer work for her and left.

Later in the week I got a call from Kent, Suzie's husband that she was at hospital in intensive care. She suffered some heavy bleeding at the base of her skull and was in a coma listed as brain dead. All the way to the hospital I prayed and talked with Suzie in my mind. I kept getting this awesome sense that she was fine, just hanging out hovering over her body and loving all those who had come to visit. As I entered the room, she looked beautiful. Even her toes were all fixed up and you couldn't tell anything was wrong except that she was in a coma-like state. There were a few friends and family and her husband Kent, but even he didn't look like he was under the usual amount of stress that accompanies these kinds of situations. There was a noticeable peace in the atmosphere around Suzie and around her loved ones.

This is not unusual for those who are prepared for death. Even those who showed up and were uncertain and very sad I noticed that very quickly they calmed down and were able to support and love each other. This is the miracle of death and transformation. Many times it brings people together and creates a sense of connection that spreads like hot butter on a warm muffin. Soon there was laughter along with the tears as memories and feelings surfaced and blended. People didn't even need encouragement to speak to Suzie as if she was listening…and I am sure she was.

Later, the next day, Kent decided to unhook life support and bid farewell to his wife of many years. I was privileged to be in the room along with 12 to 15 people as we all said goodbye as if we were seeing her off on a cruise.

There is something remarkable about this miracle of transformation. It doesn't matter your religion; the experience of peace and love is not owned by one religion. The peace and love experienced by all transcends human ideals and exposes the ultimate truth: We are all One! Religions are just a pathway to God and all paths lead to God.

I saw a statement I liked recently that said Jesus was not a Christian, Buddha was not a Buddhist, and Mohammed was not a Muslim. They were teachers of Love and that was their mission on earth.

Learn the Law of Cause and Effect

All of life is a play of two great internal movements: Cause and Effect. Cause is invisible. Effect is visible. Effect is everything you can hear, see, smell, taste, touch and physically feel. The *invisible* is the power of life energizing the belief that is creating the *visible* form. The invisible is like electricity. You can't see electricity, but when you plug in your toaster, you trust it's there. This is the same as your breath. You can't see your breath, but you know that it animates and gives life to what you feel and experience.

Without breath there is no life! With breath there is life! Life with breath is always taking form in your thoughts, in your feelings, and in your reactions. Life is made from things we can't see. This is the meaning of the famous bible quote…faith is the substance of things hoped for, the evidence of things not seen (Hebrews 11:1). The *invisible* nature of life is everywhere and the things that don't breathe vibrate. The Universe is in a constant state of vibration. This is Cause animating form and energizing life. Even as Suzie lay on her bed brain dead but breathing, she was still tethered to her form. The moment they removed the tubes and medication she stopped breathing and moved out of a physical condition bound by space, time and duration into a spiritual reality unbound and free to take whatever form she believed herself to be. Cause is forever energizing life, taking form, then discarding form and taking on new form. This, in part, explains that famous bit of wisdom, "In my Father's house there are many mansions." This is the mystery, but it is not unknown. In the physical form we tend to identify ourselves by things like our conditions, relationships, circumstances, and talents. When those things disappear, it's not unusual to feel lost. This is what grief is on the physical side of being. Briefly we are disconnected, off line, evicted. For just a moment the unknown feels real. This is when fear begins to rise. Something is not right. There is a mental vacuum. The Universe abhors a vacuum. It doesn't take long before the internal and the Infinite begin to set up shop and re-form our lives. This is the miracle of life on both sides of the curtain. This is not noticed by many. It is just one of those consistencies that are true for all of creation.

As we pass through this form, we gain knowledge and build consciousness—the awareness of life that gives us freedom and motivation to live constructive and productive lives.

Patty P.

Beautiful, courageous, assertive and loyal—these are the words that describe the charismatic nature of Patty P. When I met Patty P., she was married to Tony, a good friend who passed away unexpectedly from bone cancer. Patty P., like all of us, was saddened and shocked by Tony's sudden departure, but her grief was burdened by the discovery that she had ALS, also known as Lou Gehrig's disease.

Patty took my wife and me to lunch one afternoon and told us that she had been diagnosed with ALS and was given two years to live. She then immediately started planning and going on many cruises and trips. The terrible nature of ALS was not immediately obvious. The only symptom was her lack of balance and weakness. Gradually, her condition worsened, and in a few short years she was too weak to walk and drove her SUV around with a portable scooter-like vehicle that she unloaded herself. Then one day, she couldn't drive and was mostly staying at home. It was then, that my wife, Patty, who was one of Patty P's good friends, decided to start visiting her every Monday. This went on for at least three more years. About every third or fourth time, I went with my wife, and it was always a celebration. Patty P. would have her caregiver prepare lunch for us, and when we arrived, the first thing we had to do was eat dessert first.

Patty P. had decided to not limit her joy at our visits and insisted that we share all about our lives. She wanted to know all the gossip and intrigue and was always a loyal supporter who was more interested in caring for us than wanting any sympathy or attention for herself. Every day, she did some sort of spiritual practice. She was always reminding me that her courage was the result of her spiritual education and that she was blessed to have so many friends and loved ones who regularly visited her and brought her much joy and love.

Patty P. went on to live six-years, and over a period of time lost her ability to eat, walk, talk, and breathe, but I rarely heard her complain or give up. When she passed, she had a wonderful memorial at Soka University in their founder's hall at which I officiated. Hundreds of us gathered in her memory and told stories of her courage and inspirational nature. We laughed, we cried, we hugged, and we reminded ourselves of what it meant to live a life of love, service, and peace.

Patty P. took six years to transform herself into the angel that slowly emerged the weaker she became. Her life inspired all whom she knew. But this was no accident or anomaly. Patty P. trained herself to be spiritually attentive and was a great example of what it means to be spiritually mature. When you have the tools that help you transform, you help all those around you transform. As Winston Churchill once said, "A rising tide lifts all ships."

Learn to love and trust the life you've been given to live

Love and trust are the gold standard of knowledge. If you build your trust in life and learn to move with love through all the adventures your journey of life provides, you will find a depth of faith which will translate your mentality into the most precious and illuminating diamond you can possibly imagine. You've probably heard of those who have died and returned to tell about the light that beckoned them into heaven. This light becomes you're here-and-now light which enlightens the way through the mutual fears we share and reveals the miracle of the lives we've been given to live.

Like Patty P., our spiritual practice matures and we become the lover we have been in search of all our lives.

To those who have yet to find this life I am writing about, do not fear. It is as close as your next prayer. Your affirmative voice lifted in faith announcing the blessing of love and becoming the lover you so admire reveals the real freedom we are all seeking. As a colleague of mine once said, "God is Big Sweetie and all you need remember is the three letters that spell the work *ask*: A is for Ask—ask and it shall be answered, S is for Seek—seek and you shall find, K is for Knock—Knock and the door will be opened." Life is what you think it is and that is both the blessing and the challenge.

"If I had no sense of humor, I would long ago have committed suicide."
– **Mahatma Gandhi**

"Suicide is a permanent solution to a temporary problem."
– **Phil Donohue, NBC TV, May 23, 1984**

Chapter 7
Suicide

The Truth about Suicide

Assisted or self-inflicted, suicide is a choice driven by unbearable emotional and physical pain. It is a feeling of not being able to connect enough dots to feel like you want to be present in the world. But there is a difference between *assisted* suicide and *self-inflicted* suicide.

Assisted suicide is done with the knowledge and understanding that there is no cure for the particular disease the patient has, and that they have chosen to leave their bodies to avoid a catastrophic decline in their physical and/or mental abilities. In fact, most doctors die at home because they know that all hospitals have a policy that says they must keep-you-alive-at-all-costs. No matter how much suffering the patient endures, doctors will say they took an oath to keep you alive and that there are drugs which can help you manage your pain and discomfort while you wait to die.

Do Not Resuscitate ~ Jan's Story

In the mid-90s I had a member of my congregation who had gone blind in her teens and was so inspired to help others that in her mid-60s she took three years of classes to become a prayer practitioner. Jan never let her condition get in the way of her life. She showed up every week, completed her class work, and served many, using affirmative prayer to help them through their fear, disbelief and troubles.

Just two years into her prayer practitioner work, Jan was diagnosed with stomach cancer and went into the hospital for an operation. She knew the seriousness of her condition and had a medical directive to not keep her alive with any machines, drugs, or procedures.

Suicide

I was at the hospital just after she came out of surgery and went into the critical care recovery room. When I got to her she was hooked up to a breathing device that was forcing air into her lungs, had a tube down her throat to drain fluids out of her lungs and was being given drugs to keep up her blood pressure.

When I asked the nurse if this was part of her recovery, she said, "No, we don't expect her to survive because they didn't get all the cancer in her stomach."

Then I realized that she was conscious and could hear me. I held her hand and asked her to squeeze it if she wanted to be disconnected from these devices. She squeezed very hard and moved her head the direction of my voice. I stayed and assured her I would talk to the doctors and let them know her wishes.

It took about 30 minutes before all of her kids could get the hospital and we stood in the hallway and discussed her condition. All agreed she did not want to be hooked up to these machines and taking these drugs.

Finally we went into a room next to Jan's room and spoke with her doctors. They said they were unaware of her advanced medical directive and were bound by hospital policy to keep her alive. It took 20 more minutes to find the paperwork in her file and a staff member brought it into the room.

Time to Leave

Almost immediately, one of the nurses left the room and removed the blood pressure medication. Jan slipped into a coma and when I walked into the room they were removing the drainage tube in her lungs and turned off the breathing machine.

She stopped breathing and departed this world.

The Self-Inflicted Suicide ~ Three Case Studies

The self-inflicted suicide is without the consent of the patient's loved ones because the patient has *isolated* themselves in their condition. Alone and frustrated by their inability to find a life worth living, they take the path of least resistance and depart.

Depression, post traumatic shock disorders, and different types of mental illnesses are self-absorbing jungles, not always obvious, even to the patient. Some get lost; some will find their way home; some will commit suicide.

But the common denominator I observe in those who stay away from suicide is a well-integrated philosophical compass that guides them to their emotional north. Those who lack this *internal* compass remain isolated in their personality and can't find a life worth living.

The assisted suicide is supported by loving friends and family who celebrate the departure.

Those who commit self-inflicted suicide escape their pain, but leave their friends and loved ones struggling to understand how they could have missed the symptoms or kept them from self-destruction.

The only way to heal the wound of guilt is to forgive the choice and find a way to celebrate what was good and worthwhile about their loved one's life. When you acknowledge the good, it's easier to release them to their on-going journey into a greater experience of love. This is the only way I have observed that brings closure to the wound and releases the survivor to move forward with their lives.

Case Studies *(the names have been changed and some details altered)*

Randle

Randle was a college graduate and smart, but rarely present, even when he was around you. In class, Randle nodded his head, but struggled to grasp the lessons. "I just want to make money," he'd say.

"How about you find a way to be happy," I muttered under my breath. Randle had a dangerous kind of street smarts, the kind where you can't afford to lose.

He never felt satisfied. Randle struggled to find a relationship. He liked sex and he liked drugs. We talked, I did some prayer work for him and for a while it looked like he was going to change. Then he disappeared and I heard from a member on my staff that he was asking them for help. This went on for about a year. Once in a while he would show up for a Sunday service. Then he stopped showing up. About a year or so later I heard from his mother. "Randle killed himself."

You can't always help those who are at risk. If they get lost in their failed expectations, it's easy to conceal their pain and minimize the danger.

As the wheels come off of their awareness, they get trapped in their agony and try to ease their unhappiness by taking drugs or drinking alcohol. This can initiate a sequence of events that can lead to suicide. When you lose your grip and you start to slip, you can't stop the landslide.

Gloria

Gloria was an older congregant and part of my first ministry. She had been in love but her relationship ended abruptly. She called to get some prayer work and never mentioned suicide and I didn't get the impression it was on the table. We talked briefly and I did the prayer work and she seemed okay for a few weeks. Then one of her friends called and said she had been drinking and closed the garage door and started her car. They found her the next day.

I felt a great sadness and wondered if I had done all I could have done to prevent her suicide. I called a friend of mine, a retired psychologist who volunteered for years as a suicide hotline operator. She listened to my story, then said; "You did all you could. She was *spiritual* when she was sober and *human* when she was drinking. You can't be responsible for an alcoholic who drank themselves into a corner that had only one way out."

I remembered a wisdom I learned in Alanon and that part of the Serenity Prayer attributed to Reinhold Neibuhr: *God, grant me the serenity to accept the things I cannot change. The courage to change the things I can, and the wisdom to know the difference.*

With every experience of this type you grow a little more observant. It takes time to learn the signs of struggle. Now, when I see that inner-battle, I shift my attention to an even greater idea of love and hold that person in perfect peace. It is not up to me to change their minds. But it is up to me change my mind about their spiritual presence and make sure that they see me as an ally and not someone who judges them in any way shape or form. This has made a difference in others that I have been able to help.

Ed

Ed was a proud man. He wasn't a regular. He was ex-military and border-line rude. "I don't need prayers," he said to me.

"Okay," I said. Then about a year later Ed's girlfriend called, "Ed killed himself."

"Why?" I asked.

"He was convicted of fraud and was going to prison for two years. He drove himself into the wilderness and shot himself."

"I'm sorry," I said. "I liked Ed."

His girlfriend was quiet. I heard her take a breath and exhale these words through her tears, "Thank you Dr. Jim. He liked you too."

I share these stories with you because we can't always fix the ones we love. That doesn't mean we stop trying. There is only one mind we can change, our own. We can't change the mind of another, but we can lead them to the well, and if they're thirsty they will drink—or not drink.

Just because someone commits suicide does not mean we have to view their lives as a failure. People who commit suicide have lost touch with being alive, and they can't find their spiritual compass and even if you placed it in their hands, they wouldn't know how use it to find their way home.

I remember a forest ranger who was giving a talk about being lost in the wilderness. "Most people walk in circles, stay lost, get dehydrated and die. Some, however, will remember my advice." He paused and looked each one of us in the eye, then said, "If you get lost, sit in an open area and wait to be found."

I've walked a lot of people out of the cave of despair. But a few were in a room so lost they could not find themselves nor was there enough light in their hearts to see the opportunity of the life they had been given to live. They wouldn't wait in an open area for help. They became *spiritually dehydrated* and died from a self-inflicted sense of failure and hopelessness.

Does suicide make death a different experience?

There are many speculations about suicide and the consequence in the afterlife. Most in the western world of religion sees suicide as a sin that has penalties that vary from an extended stay in purgatory to an eternal stay in hell, or an afterlife in a sort of a suspended sleep awaiting love's true kiss to be awakened.

I don't believe any of those are true, but I do believe that you are accountable and must keep working on your "consciousness" to accumulate enough capacity to love the life you've been created to live and eliminate the necessity for any kind of self-inflicted end.

The presence of God's Love is always seeking expression by means of your *soul*. Those who have no connection with their soul struggle to allow love into their lives. They are captivated by a *low curiosity* that keeps them contained in their personality. They are prisoners in a jail of discontent, distracted by the human conditions of anger, fear, and blame.

If you are caught up in this loop of hopelessness, stuck in a pattern of failure and limitation, it's only a matter of time until your circumstances will surround you and offer you a way out. But don't be fooled. Seek help and get some counseling that can provide a different philosophical answer.

For those who have suffered the loss of a loved one and are still trying to figure out why

Before I offer you my counsel I would like to say, "I am sorry for your loss. If you are still grieving because you do not understand why, I want you to know that my prayers are with you and that there is a power within you that can heal your unhappiness if you will allow it to heal the way you think."

The death of a loved one by suicide is one of the most difficult losses you will ever experience. The mind of the loved one who took their own life, without your permission or knowledge, was not focused on you. It was focused on themselves and their condition. They became lost in a world of options that went blank and were not receptive to any other thoughts.

Those who work in suicide prevention know that the mind of the one at risk must be distracted and turned away from the thought of suicide. But for some, there will come a time when their thinking will overwhelm them and push them into a corner with only one exit.

The truth about those who commit suicide is that it has nothing to do with the loved ones left devastated by the act. The answer as to why lives only in the mind of the one who committed suicide, and you do not have access to that mind. Thus, speculation is pointless and will not help you heal the loss.

This does not mean that you won't speculate, it means that you have chosen to live in peace and accept that your departed loved one is also at peace and fully aware of the corrections that must be made. Death is departure and the destination for all is God.

I offer these three affirmations that can help you regain your spiritual balance and embrace your feelings and heal your thoughts.

1. In this moment I claim God's guidance and release my speculation. I dwell only on the sacred and see my departed loved one as whole, perfect and complete.
2. God's way is always love and peace. I chose both as my way and the way of the Divine. I am healed of any doubt and I dismiss all and any thoughts that would rob me of my eternal peace of mind.
3. The Universe has a plan—Love. I am in and of this Universe of Love and see my path as God's path. Thank you God for all my blessings.

A Philosophy of Healing

People who commit suicide do so because they were unable to control the conditions they encountered. They could only view their world from their *human personality.* They didn't have a way of thinking that could shine the light in a different direction. This is why a Spiritual Philosophy is important.

If you struggle with this problem, find a counselor as fast as you can. If you can't afford a counselor, find a minister who can help you see your life from a different point of view.

One immediate way to change your mind is to focus on a Principle like love and keep asking yourself these questions:

1. Is there someone in my life I could serve and love? If there isn't, what non-profit could use my help?
2. What am I missing?
3. If love was a person what would love tell me to do?
4. How would I help another if they were having my problem?

We all have moments of vulnerability and we all have moments of weakness. Would you be willing to ask someone for prayer work? If so, what, exactly, would you ask for?

For instance, would you be willing to ask a minister to pray for your peace of mind and enthusiasm for living life?

If you've lost a loved one to suicide

If they have taken their own lives, forgive them. They did not know what they were doing. Instead, celebrate their passing and know that they did not die. Their spirits have reformed on the *other side* and they are still and will be forever creative beings of light, love and peace.

One definition of a healing is you can't remember the pain, the fear, or the condition. This may seem impossible when it comes to suicide. How can you not remember the anger, guilt, and shame when a friend or loved one commits suicide? These are common and powerful reactions memorized and held in the subconscious by humanity, but they can be neutralized, deconstructed and released. One way is to understand that a reaction is something you're passing through, not making a career out of. A powerful affirmation that helps to neutralize the reaction is, "This too shall pass," followed with another affirmation, "Love casts out all fear."

These kinds of affirmations help to calm the subconscious and neutralize the reactions by redirecting our feelings with a more powerful way to think and react. I consider these types of comments miracle words because they are effective and they work.

The national suicide hot line which is available 24/7 is **1 (800) 273-8255** and it is FREE.

Suicide

One day we will all be together. There is no death! Only eternal life! Please, love the life you've been given to live.

"A great soul serves everyone all the time. A great soul never dies. It brings us together again and again."
—**Maya Angelou**

Chapter 8
The Memorial, The Memory, The Miracle

Who is the memorial for?

Almost everyone assumes that the memorial is for departed. It is not. The memorial is an important part of the grieving process. It is a formality that puts a *period* on a life that has transformed so family and friends can move on.

It's not unusual for a patient to say, "I don't want a fuss when I die. It's a waste of money. Why cause all that suffering. It's such an inconvenience."

Time to Leave

My first ministry was in Cape Coral, Florida. This was a community on the gulf side of the state made up mostly of retired folks. Most of my congregants had relatives who lived out of state. I did a lot of memorials and many relatives traveled long distances to attend. The point is, the memorial is for the living, not the dead. It is the opportunity to heal the sense of loss and reconcile the internal confusion that takes time, love, and acceptance to restore to balance.

If you follow the historical experience of humanity and how most cultures handle death, there is a consistent record of ceremony and celebration. Cultures and religions of all kinds find value in taking time to remember and celebrate their loved ones.

If you are the patient, please consider the importance of a memorial. Let your loved ones honor you so they can heal their sense of separation and get on with their lives. Consider the benefit to the younger generation. They are afforded the opportunity to hear stories about generosity, dealing with hard times, and the courage it takes to forgive and understand what motivates the human condition. This is valuable information that shapes lives and can play a part in determining destiny.

The unresolved feelings that can dwell in the heart are a part of the ongoing problem of unexpressed grief and could have been resolved if there had been an opportunity to understand the family dynamics that are often revealed at memorials.

It still surprises me that many lives are not as transparent as you think. People often say to me at the reception after the memorial, *I had no idea that happened, I didn't know they had an interest in that, why didn't they tell me.* Even I find out things that surprise me, of which the most surprising is how secretive people are about helping others. Most people are humble and don't want credit for helping others. If you are one of those who don't want the information about your generosity revealed, think of the good that results when the revelation of that information inspires others to follow your lead. Sometimes goodness needs a little more transparency so others can learn what it means to be good.

What needs to happen at the memorial?

Memorials are like operas. They have sadness, laughter, tears, and death. They are rich and important plays that help us complete the picture of the dearly departed. They are cathartic opportunities that give us a chance to release the pent-up emotions brought to the surface. Many old dinosaurs rise out of our mental caves, and we feel them in our throats and guts choking our breath. After all, it is the nature of Spirit to breathe, and when we struggle to breathe, it jams us into a spiritual context that, for a moment, we cannot escape. We are *prisoners of the moment.* This is how the *now* captures our attention and unites us with what it means to be alive. What it means to lose all worry and surrender to the *present*, the Holy Spirit, and the sacred idea of life.

Memorials can start with a musical selection that helps relax our egos so we can drop our defenses. If you choose the right song it can bring the attention of those in attendance to a place of perfect unified love. In other words, most everyone is on the same emotional page. After that the minister can welcome everyone and begin with a prayer created to center us on healing our loss, opening our hearts, and releasing the dearly departed so they can get on with their lives. This is the protocol I follow. Then, what I do, is read three statements which I have put at the end of this book. The first is a statement about how God is a God of the living, not the dead. The second statement is from Gibran about death and trust. The third is the 23rd Psalm, "The Lord is my shepherd." After I've read the three statements, I then invite those who have been picked to eulogize the departed, to read from their prepared thoughts how they knew the departed and what that relationship meant to them. I always encourage written statements because it guarantees that what they wanted to say gets said and it keeps them from wandering into emotional *mind* fields. Although I can't control the length of their prepared words, I ask that they try to keep it to three typed pages, double spaced.

After the eulogies have been read, I usually invite the attendees to tell brief anecdotal stories that help complete our picture of the departed. This is where we sometimes learn things we didn't know, and a lot of laughter can come forth. Then, after six to eight people have shared, I end the sharing and encourage those who have stories left to tell, to tell them to each other.

Then I start my healing message that centers on three talking points. First, there is the necessity to release our loved ones and get on with our lives. Second, the healing of loss by focusing on how we were loved by the departed and the willingness to make a commitment to honor the memory of our loved one by loving each other as they loved us. Third, to take the opportunity to let love move us into a place of peace, forgiveness, and acceptance.

Then I give everyone about 40 seconds in silence to say good-bye. Then I signal the music, either a soloist or a recording, to play one of the departed ones favorite songs. Many times it is something like *Amazing Grace, What a Wonderful World*, or even, *Sitting on the Dock of the Bay*. Whatever is played, it always brings the attendees together, and the memorial ends on a positive feeling of devotion, departure, and a feeling of God's presence within.

The Miracle ~ 30, 60, 90, 120 Days Out

Death is a tumultuous process of growth. Normal growth is like that popular idea of *peeling back the onion*. Death *chops the onion*. There is nothing gradual about the chaos death can cause. It is an internal convulsion that disrupts your life.

My favorite analogy is *eviction*. Death kicks you out of your mental and emotional home and deprives you of the comfort of your habits and judgments. Death is a tornado: you lose power, the roof is blown away, and your life is flooded with feelings that render you hopeless.

Death, however, is not the end. It is the beginning of a miracle called "grief." I like the acronym I invented for GRIEF: God's Righteousness Inspires, Emancipates and Fulfills!

Grief is a miracle that reassembles your life and helps reconnect the dots. It is a gradual process that slowly takes you by the hand and walks you out of the *valley of the shadow of death.*

The first 30 days after the death of a loved one there is typically a lot of mental stress, confusion and, for many, a lethargic feeling of hopelessness. This is where some people get lost and need to be with someone who can reassure them *that this too shall pass.* This is a temporary experience where your internal compass has stopped working and there is a definite loss of direction. This kind of disorientation is normal and it lasts for 30 to 45 days. If it goes beyond that, you should seek counseling with a minister or therapist and/or join a grief support group. Most hospitals have grief support groups and they are usually led by trained counselors who can help walk you out of the shadow.

Sixty days after the death of a loved one most people will notice a gradual feeling of order and routine. Their depression is less frequent and their memories are sorting themselves out. It's like a storm that has kicked up a bunch of large waves that have gradually diminished in size and frequency. However, big emotional waves occasionally come out of nowhere and swamp our recovery, and for a brief period of time we may feel disoriented. This is where affirmations can help restore your equilibrium.

Time to Leave

I suggest copying one of the following affirmations on to a 3 x 5 card and carry it with you during the day. Then once every hour say the affirmation aloud. Remember, you're not trying to make the affirmation true; you are repeating it because it is true. This is an effective way to educate our subconscious mind because it establishes a narrative that can eclipse the painful messages sent by our experience of loss.

The ego, however—that human-centered repository of *will*—will attempt to swamp the boat and overturn your progress. If you have frequently repeated the affirmations below, it will keep the boat upright and you will handle the reflex emotions that are trying to flood your life.

Here are three affirmations that can help you recover your balance (or if you want, you can write your own):

1. Today I am the loving presence of God's good living at peace with a great sense of joy. The real power of life is my Faith!

2. In this moment I gather my principles of Life, Light, and Love and focus my thoughts on that that which illumines my path and animates my joy. The reality of my life is God's Love.

3. I rest in the arms of Spirit's genius and breathe in the energy of Spirit's unconditional Love. Rest is power.

90 days after your loss, life will regain momentum and a lighter and lighter feeling will begin to inform your blessings. This is the miracle of grief. Millions and millions of people are set upright in a very short time and life becomes a series of opportunities to live, create and serve. Ninety days out, it's not untypical to have powerful surges of creative energy. Take advantage of these surges. They are part of the miracle. I believe they are a gift from those we thought we had lost who are now present inspiring and guiding our growth. Remember, grief reorganizes us internally and we are suddenly aware of the gifts we have been given and are now urged to use and develop. Gifts, like patience, harmony, and an endless variety of creative ideas excite our intellects and refocus us on fulfilling our potential.

These things I write about are not usually connected to grief. Most people don't associate these surges with the passing of a loved one. Unfortunately, some will misread these signs and ignore the benefits. Like seeds of freedom, these urgings will sit dormant within awaiting our awakening, ready to spring back the moment we understand the signals they are sending. Again, very few will connect this to the passing of a loved one. Some will have dreams where they see or even talk with the departed and maybe feel their support. We just need to remember, they may have checked out but they never leave.

120 days out most are free from death's chaos and are living deliberately. This is a good time to make a list of all the things you're grateful for. It's called a gratitude list and it is important in configuring your *mindset*. This keeps you on track and moving in the direction of your greatest good. Death and transformation can now be seen as a blessing. They have moved us out of our complacency and helped us see our potential. Our loved ones are alive and functioning and we are alive and functioning, albeit on different planes, but nonetheless, we are once again engaged in being alive.

The miracle has happened. We are reorganized and internally balanced. This may not last. It may feel like a passing fancy. God, however, does not rest. 24/7 God's intelligence is guiding us, and life is signaling us to stay alert. An even greater good is in the pipe line!

"There are only two ways to live your life. One is as though nothing is a miracle. The other is as though everything is a miracle."
—**Albert Einstein**

Chapter 9
The Memorial Service

Music and introduction of immediate family

I suggest that the memorial begins with a musical selection that helps to center everyone's attention. Then I welcome all attendees to this Celebration of Life and remind all that we are here to say good-bye and celebrate love.

I usually then do a centering prayer that always starts in this fashion: However you know God to be in your heart, whatever you religious or spiritual tradition,

I ask you to bring that forward and together let us celebrate the life of _____.

Statement of Truth

"God is not a God of the dead, but of the living, for in God's sight, all are alive." The spirit is both birthless and deathless. The Principle of Life cannot know death. The experience of dying is but the laying off of an old garment and the donning of a new one. Just as there are bodies celestial and bodies terrestrial, there is a material body and a spiritual body. This spiritual body is the resurrection body.

Gibran on Death

Gibran wrote about death and said: "In the depth of your hopes and desires lies your silent knowledge of the beyond, and like a seed dreaming beneath snow, your heart dreams of spring. Trust the dreams, for in them is hidden the gate to eternity. Your fear of death is but the trembling of the shepherd when he stands before the king whose hand is to be laid upon him in honor."

The 23rd Psalm

"The Lord is my shepherd; I shall not want. He makes me to rest in green pastures; He leads me in the paths of righteousness for His name's sake. Yea, though I walk through the valley of the shadow of death, I will fear no evil; for Thou art with me; Thy rod and Thy staff they comfort me. Thou preparest a table before me in the presence of mine enemies; Thou annointest my head with oil; my cup runneth over. Surely Thy goodness and mercy shall follow me all the days of my life; and I shall dwell in the house of the Lord forever."

_____ is in the house of the Lord.

(Insert favorite Scripture to be read by a family member or a friend or comments or special song)

Eulogies, sharing and music

It is appropriate at this time to have two or three people officially eulogize the departed. I suggest two to three double-spaced pages.

Sharing takes place after the official eulogies are read. Then I ask attendees to share a brief anecdotal story that best describes how they knew the departed. I emphasize brief. When they raise their hands, I choose one person at a time, hand them a portable mic, and ask them to stand and introduce themselves. When they're done, I take the portable mic and choose another.

Time to Leave

Usually about six to 10 people will share. Then I end the sharing and suggest that those who didn't get an opportunity to speak share with each other at the reception following the memorial.

Minister's healing message

I talk about the Universal and Infinite nature of God.

I remind everyone that most spiritual traditions acknowledge that God created all of life.

I then declare a healing for the void left on the conscious level of expression.

I give thanks for the life of the departed.

I then release and affirm the nature of eternal Life.

Release

We have come today to honor the spirit and express our love for _____ and his/her eternal journey of life. We do not deny our grief, but accept it as a part of our expression of love as an act of release. We are open in our sorrow, but strong in our faith of eternal life.

Now in the silence of the moment, and for each in their own way, let us release the body but keep the memory of _____ immortal and alive, existing in a spiritual and mental atmosphere of peace and love.

(Wait 40 seconds in silence)

Closing song, prayer or ask the attendees to say the Lord's Prayer aloud.

More programs by Dr. Jim Turrell

The **Next Step Workshop** is a 60 to 90-minute three-part presentation based on Dr. Jim's book, *Time to Leave*. It's perfect for boomers and their children and families with grandparents. You will learn:

1. The Nature of Death as Transformation and a Cosmic Shove into a Greater Experience of Life.
2. Practical Tools that will prepare you for grief, death, fear, and the confusion that always accompanies the departure.
3. The Family Legacy Challenge: A way to leave a legacy that can heal, transform and enlighten future generations.

The **Family Legacy Challenge** was created to encourage parents and grandparents to complete an Identity Journal and leave it as a means for future generations to have some idea of the way they *thought* and *felt* about the world they lived in. Imagine how different it would be if you could read a journal that helped you understand how your ancestors experienced the world and what they learned and how they changed as a result? Lean more: WWW.FamilyLegacChallenge.com

Contact Information for Dr. Jim Turrell
Email: jturrell@cslnm.org ~ Office Phone: 714 754-7399

Made in the USA
San Bernardino, CA
13 August 2015